A Victim of Boards of Directors

Noie James
A Victim of Boards of Directors

BASED ON A TRUE STORY

iUniverse, Inc.
Bloomington

A Victim of Boards of Directors
Based on a True Story

iUniverse books may be ordered through booksellers or by contacting:

iUniverse
1663 Liberty Drive
Bloomington, IN 47403
www.iuniverse.com
1-800-Authors (1-800-288-4677)

ISBN: 978-1-4620-6145-7 (sc)
ISBN: 978-1-4620-6146-4 (ebk)

Printed in the United States of America

iUniverse rev. date: 10/21/2011

INTRODUCTION

For sixteen years, I have pursued every opportunity available to me to restore my reputation and good name. They mean everything to me.

I wrote this book in the hope of settling my dispute with two non-profit organizations and the Chief Executive Officer (CEO).

The Board of Directors manages one of the organizations through a Policy Governance Structure that allows the CEO to work with a great deal of autonomy.

According to a past Chair of the first organization, "The principles and boundaries of policy governance allow the Board to take a futuristic strategic direction and not get caught up in the detail . . . of operations." This is not necessarily a good thing if the management team is dishonest.

It has been my experience that the CEO is free to inform the Boards of Directors whatever she wants to communicate without question. She chooses what to tell the directors and what not to tell them. This works well for the directors, who are able to claim ignorance when serious problems arise. The CEO is also a member of the second organization's Board of Directors.

When the CEO committed crimes of fraud and lying under oath, the Boards of Directors ignored the evidence of her wrongdoings. Instead, they decided to support her no matter what the cost.

It is appropriate to say that the directors don't want to know what the CEO has done wrong. They have been sent an enormous amount of proof; yet, they have chosen to remain silent.

CHAPTER ONE

The CEO's white collar crimes of fraud and lying under oath (during the Examination for Discovery) have been supported by the Boards of Directors of both organizations and two sponsors without question.

The details of the crimes committed by the CEO have been repeatedly reported to the respective Boards of Directors. To date, all of the directors have chosen to ignore her criminal wrongdoings.

Over the past sixteen years, I have contacted 71 directors of four Boards of Directors to try to clear my name. The directors and executives have never responded to my correspondence.

Background

In September 1992, I accepted the position of the Director of Finance and Administration with the first organization.

As Director of Finance and Administration, my responsibilities included: development and management of the human resources required for administrative and financial reporting functions; development and overseeing procedures for administrative functions, including human resource policies for the organization; maintenance and management of the associations' technology information systems; overseeing the preparation of an annual budget of two million dollars; development and management of the association's facility; coordination of the production of the association's bilingual journal; and administrative duties for the second organization.

In June 1994, I quit my job as Director of Finance and Administration to take over as Project Manager for two major projects for the two organizations. I signed two fixed price contracts, **60374** and **72850**. The two contracts expired March 31, 1995. I also had a third contract with another company for over $90.000.00. The company has since gone out of business. My business grossed over $183,000.00 in my first fifteen months of operations.

Each contract specified the responsibilities of the named staff. I was required to submit monthly project reports to the CEO. These reports consisted of the current status updates for current tasks and recommendations for future tasks to be completed. Where appropriate, recommendations included alternative courses of action and selection of vendors.

CHAPTER TWO

Under contract **60374**, I worked with five people in a Working Group that reported to representatives of eight provinces and the CEO. The small Working Group's assignment was to develop a national membership administrative system to support the new association after the provincial and national associations merged into one organization.

The process for the Working Group required me to take the lead in drafting documents such as the Master Plan of Action and Policy Document. The drafts would be discussed briefly at one hour teleconference meetings and would be reviewed in depth at a later date. Based on the feedback from the members of the Working Group, the documents were modified and then distributed to the full team for comment.

With respect to the membership contract, the CEO's claim that the staff had to rework some of the tasks that I was responsible for makes no sense given the details of my Letter of Engagement.

The Policy Document was prepared in the same manner that previous major documents had been prepared, such as the Master Plan of Action. The Plan was used to monitor the status of individual assignments and highlight problems. Administrative and accounting procedures had been delayed and deadlines were repeatedly extended. Information about the delays was provided to the CEO on an ongoing basis since October 1994, verbally and in writing. The CEO's claim that tasks had to be reworked is a conundrum, since it is not possible to rework something that has not been started, such as the creation of generic membership materials.

To prepare the draft Policy Document, the starting point was to review the notes from a discussion with the CEO on September 14, 1994. She specified the information that should be included in the document. I then contacted each provincial representative to obtain feedback on the April 5, 1995 project update. I was responsible for the following tasks:

1. reviewing all relevant documentation in the project files going back to February 1994;
2. following up with all provincial representatives to determine if there were any new concerns which needed to be addressed;
3. incorporating into the Policy Document the Ontario provincial organization's performance requirements as described by the Executive Director;
4. updating the Master Plan of Action;
5. drafting a document that put into writing the expectations of all of the provincial organizations; and
6. obtaining feedback on a proposed evaluation process.

These types of documents had always been sent out a couple of days before the Working Group meetings. They could not be reviewed in depth at any meetings because we only had one hour.

Given the facts that there were no precedents to work with, that at some point I would be replaced as Project Coordinator, that it would take at least three months to reach a consensus on the document, and just as with the Master Plan of Action, the Policy Document would have to be revised, it is absurd and malicious for the CEO to describe my work as incomplete, deficient, of little value and not coordinated with other aspects of the project.

There was no reason to delay drafting the Policy Document. There were important reasons to prepare the draft in June 1995, including: 1) the amount of time that had elapsed since the project had started (close to eighteen months), 2) the pending resignation of one member of the Working Group on June 30, 1995, 3) two associations still not having committed to participation in the new system, and 4) an Executive Director having to make a presentation about the new system to her Board of Directors on June 23rd. She did not have the benefit of knowing much about the work that had been done over the last year.

In preparation for the June 14, 1995 teleconference meeting, I had couriered documents to the CEO on June 9th. She did not respond to my letter. I arrived at the first organization's office prepared to chair the meeting. The Ontario association's Executive Director informed me that the CEO had cancelled the meeting. The CEO made no attempt to talk to me while she and I were in the office. She did not advise me that she had terminated my work or that she had any concerns until she wrote to me on June 21st. There were no follow-up activities for me to handle, since the meeting never took place.

The June 21st, letter deliberately gives the impression that she was completely unaware that her staff were not handling their part of the work on the project. The CEO's actions and statements were oppressive. Withholding fees that were rightfully owed to me and my company was done with malice and completely in bad faith.

She deliberately misrepresented the facts in her June 21st letter. The letter's purpose was simply meant to be a justification for her malicious actions. At no time, did I tender my resignation for the membership project.

Per the Master Plan of Action, the project was not scheduled to be completed until some time in 1997. I never agreed to work on the Policy Document until the end of the project. There was nothing for anyone to rework, since I had started with a blank slate and according to the CEO, her staff were not knowledgeable about the work the Group was doing after eighteen months of working on the project. Even though the June 14th meeting would have been the fifth teleconference meeting of the Working Group, the CEO wrote that her staff "*. . . could not explain to*" her "*the expected outcome*" of the meeting. Because the meeting was only an hour long, no one individual could speak for much more than five minutes. According to the CEO, her staff could not even do that.

On April 24, 1995, I sent information to two staff members relating to the development of generic association materials. On June 12th, I was advised that neither individual had even looked at the materials.

The CEO's claim that the draft Policy Document prepared by me had little value and no merit, was made in bad faith, with respect to not paying my full invoice for the work. This document was a first draft on which the team could build. The information was not documented anywhere else. New members were being added to the Working Group and the provincial representatives' team. This document was their introduction to the status of the project. This also meant that the Master Plan of Action had to be updated for the third time.

The national membership system project was on schedule for those tasks that I and two provincial representatives were responsible for handling. Monthly project status reports identified those tasks which were behind schedule. Problems with the first organization's administrative staff and managers were repeatedly discussed with the CEO. She never addressed the problems of incompetence and procrastination satisfactorily.

The teleconference meeting had originally been scheduled for May 29, 1995. The staff confirmed that they were ready for the meeting. It had to be rescheduled to June 14th, due to the unavailability of the British Columbia member of the group. The CEO cancelled the meeting without notice and wrote me a self-serving letter which I took to be the termination of my services.

The work process that I followed from the start of the membership system project was to send out the agendas a few days before the meetings along with any documents to be discussed. After the meetings, the group members would take a couple of weeks to review the materials and get back to me with their comments and completed assignments. Then the information would be distributed to the whole team for comments and questions. This process had worked well until June 9th.

CHAPTER THREE

The first organization had to replace its computer system. The project involved developing a computer system that had limited access for the provincial associations and the second organization. Under contract **72850,** I was in charge of finding a suitable software application. I managed the process of gathering information on user requirements for functional specifications, selecting a vendor to develop the new computer system and negotiation of a Software Development Agreement. The Functional Specifications document and Agreement specified in detail the deliverables for the system developer. I recommended a developer and the CEO hired the company to program a custom application for the association for $50,000.00.

My job was primarily to monitor the work of the programmers to ensure that the functional requirements were met and that deadlines were on schedule. I was also the contact for thirteen staff members.

As Project Manager for the computer system project between June 27, 1994 through May 11, 1995, I was responsible for:

1. verifying the accuracy of all invoices, i.e., ensuring duplicate invoices were not paid and that separate invoices for work covered by the developer's contract were not paid;

2. working with the computer programmers up to nine hours a day. (This was necessitated by the fact that when the developers moved their office, the Entity Relation Diagram was lost.) Consequently, it was necessary to explain to the programmers on a daily basis the functionality required by the three organizations. At one point, the system had been programmed in a way that required the accounting staff to perform part of their work processing membership renewals manually. I worked with the senior programmer to re-program the system at no extra cost to the first organization;

3. meeting with three organizations' staff in groups and individually regarding reports they had requested (in excess of 40). Many hours of work were required because it turned out that while the staff wanted dozens of reports, they did not know how to formulate SQL statements and they could not identify what results they wanted to see on the reports. For example, a request was made for a report that would have printed out the entire database, when in fact the individual only wanted the names of a dozen or so members;

4. resolving complaints and researching solutions to problems and alternative ways to provide the functionality the organizations needed to have in order for the national membership system to function as required;

5. arranging for IT experts to give advice about technical issues and develop ad hoc solutions, e.g., meeting with the manager of the second organization and a specialist on local area networks to determine how to link her database to the national database;

6. following up daily with the developer regarding the status of the report software which did not work, and meeting with two new programmers that were hired on April 5, 1995;

7. writing comprehensive monthly project reports as well as other interim reports as required. Reports included the status of all pending tasks, recommendations for resolving problems, alternatives for completing tasks in the most economical way (including using other vendors instead of my company), and plans for system support in both the short and long-term; and

8. resolving staff performance issues daily, (many were related to the staff's lack of experience working in a Windows environment, lack of time to complete their regular work and train on the new system at the same time, and inadequate training delivered by the developer's System Analyst). These were several issues that caused me to withdraw my first proposal for service contract **72167** submitted to the CEO on April 3, 1995.

Per my contractual obligations, I provided monthly progress reports on the status of both projects. On March 9, 1995, I produced a report on the computer system project. I outlined different courses of action the CEO could take with regard to the future support for the new computer system. I provided a résumé for David Marsh as a potential System Analyst for the CEO's consideration.

On April 3, 1995, I gave my notice about terminating my job as Project Manager for the computer system project. The project report dated March 31, 1995 was attached. I also included a proposal to provide a System Analyst to support the computer system and users. This proposal was the first copy of contract **72167**.

On April 24th, I rescinded my contract proposal. I discussed my concerns with the CEO on April 25th in her office and agreed to submit a revised proposal for contract **72167**. I signed this second proposal on May 8th in her office.

I was led to believe that my contract would be executed. I hired a full-time System Analyst to support the staff. After I signed my contract, the CEO and I attended a staff meeting to introduce my analyst and explain his role in supporting three non-profit organizations.

When the CEO took over as Project Manager on May 12, 1995, she asked me to help her by providing numerous reports on outstanding issues, such as which reports the developer was still contractually obligated to provide and by handling some loose ends, including staff questions and billing problems. Had I known that the contract was not going to be executed, I would have billed for my time and that of my System Analyst who worked full-time. I worked over one hundred hours free based on the belief that my service contract **72167** had been executed. The CEO defrauded me and my company by waiting until May 30th to inform me that she did not intend to execute the contract. I had already invoiced the first organization for $3,000.00 assuming the contract had been executed. Later, the CEO refused to pay for the work on a time and materials basis.

CHAPTER FOUR

The CEO and I did not come to an agreement on the new computer system contract. On April 24, 1995 I wrote to her rescinding my proposal. I also wrote her a project update itemizing problems the staff were having with training on the new computer system.

The CEO lied when she wrote that she "*did not have discussions with" me" between April 24, 1995 and May 1, 1995.*" The CEO "*was not available during that period except for April 25, 1995. On this date other activities precluded the*" CEO "*from having discussions with . . .*" me.

On April 25th, I met with the CEO in her office in the evening. We discussed the problems with the staff training. She wrote out a training plan for herself and all of the staff. She gave the handwritten plan to me and accepted my recommendation to have one of the programmers train the staff. The plan was typed by the Business Manager at 8:30 a.m. on April 26th and training began at 9:00 a.m.

We also discussed my reasons for rescinding my contract proposal. We agreed on revisions and I prepared a second version of contract **72167**, which I signed on May 8, 1995 at the CEO's request.

By April 24th, the computer software developer had fallen behind in developing the database application and programming standard reports which had been identified by me and were detailed in the Functional Specification document. The project was seriously over budget and development software had to be upgraded, causing a great deal of rework for the programmers.

On May 11, 1995, the CEO and I met with the president of the system developer's company to discuss a project deficiency report. The report that we met to discuss included information on 1) existing system deficiencies, 2) the vendor's outstanding contractual obligations and 3) issues and concerns related to the quality of the developer's services. The outcome of the meeting was that the CEO agreed to allow the developer to go over budget.

The developer invoiced the first organization an additional $106,387.18 for: programming the source code, system enhancements, debugging the completed application, general support and training

In addition, the CEO wrote a letter to me on May 30th stating that ". . . We did make the decision to install the new version of forms software and we did have the subcontractors redo all the forms in the system." **It is important to note that I was not involved in any of these decisions, nor did they have anything to do with my performance as Project Manager.**

The Project Report is a follows:

IMPLEMENTATION OF DATABASE MANAGEMENT SYSTEM APPLICATION AND LOCAL AREA NETWORK

Date: May 8, 1995

Client:

Vendor:

Consultant:

I. Project Deficiencies

As of May 5, 1995, the AMS could not be accepted by the client due to the existence of the following deficiencies:

(a) *The Inventory Order Entry form does not allow users to enter "Ship To" or "Bill To" addresses for orders. At the present time, the client is unable to use this function.*

(b) *The LAN installation is incomplete and to date has not worked satisfactorily. AccPac has not been installed on the network. Staff are able to print from WordPerfect 6.1 by way of a temporary fix that has been implemented. This needs to be resolved on a permanent basis. Items B2 through B11 under LAN REQUIREMENTS on pages two and three of the fax dated March 19th need to be completed and/ or demonstrated to be working.*

(c) *Reports cannot be run from the Report Router.*

(d) *Thirty reports have not been completed and of these, work has not begun on twenty-nine.*

(e) *A User Guide for the AMS has not been delivered to the client. There was no user documentation available to staff during acceptance testing. This made it difficult for the staff to test the system effectively and has prolonged the system testing.*

(f) *The acceptance testing has not demonstrated to the CEO and designated consultants that the AMS software is performing at least adequately for the client to sufficiently use the AMS software for its operational requirements.*

(g) *The training provided by the developer was not provided to a level where: (1) the Licensed Software could be demonstrated to operate as intended by the Functional Specifications, or (2) the staff could use the AMS software for its operational requirements.*

(h) *Data cannot be exported to the client's accounting system.*

ACTIONS

(i) *The developer must provide the client with a written plan to correct the deficiencies. The developer must restore the capability for the client to resume its normal business operations within a timeframe that is acceptable to the client and at no extra cost. At the present time, the organization is not able to operate effectively and will not accept further delays in getting the AMS up and running. Effective immediately, the client will begin documenting the cost of damages which are the direct result of the developer's substandard implementation.*

(ii) The developer must provide a report from Oracle that the recent upgrade has been installed correctly and that it should have resolved the current problems with generating WordPerfect merge reports.

II. Outstanding Contractual Obligations

The developer is obligated to perform or deliver the following per the Software Development and License Agreement:

(a) demonstrate that the back-up is performing adequately.

(b) demonstrate that the AMS software performs the functions described under each menu item in Section 7 of Schedule "B" to the Agreement.

(c) demonstrate that the AMS provides the data tables and data searches for two variables.

(d) demonstrate a response time of less than 5 seconds for data searches for two variables.

(e) demonstrate a response time of less than 5 minutes for the generation of reports which utilize two tables (maximum three pages).

(f) demonstrate that all reports described in the Functional Specification can be run and printed.

(g) demonstrate that the AMS provides effective linkages (export of data) to the client's accounting system (AccPac).

(h) provide a detailed set of AMS software documentation:

- *system administrator's guide*
- *user guide which meets specifications identified in the Agreement*

- *a copy of the source code of the AMS computer program, including: (i) file and database design structure, (ii) data dictionary, (iii) input/output design and (iv) program listings (hard and soft copies).*

III. Performance Issues and concerns

The overall implementation of the AMS project has not been handled satisfactorily. The resolution of ongoing problems has been costly and time consuming for both the developer and the client. It has been hard for the staff to plan their time and much of the work performed each day has consisted of fighting fires at the last minute. The difficulties that the client has encountered are summarized below and generally relate to the quality of the developer's project management and inadequate training.

Project Management

The implementation of this project has been rushed and has suffered from attempts to take short cuts. This is true for both the development work and the installation of the LAN. Decisions such as the one to deliver the AMS much too early caused confusion and disrupted the client's operations unnecessarily. When the application was delivered, it was not useable and hardware could not be made available for both development work and training services.

You have not met the requirement for semi-monthly reports and three reports which were provided did not accurately reflect the status of this project. Many problems which should have been identified and brought to the client's attention were addressed much too late or not at all. These include the delay in starting development work on reports, the loss of documentation needed by the programmers, and your staffing shortage. In addition, your decision to change the plan presented in its project report without consulting the client was an unacceptable way of trying to make up time on the project.

It does not appear that much of the work required to complete this project has been carried out according to a well thought out plan. For example, it has been difficult to obtain timely information about tasks which needed to be handled by the staff, such as the table updates. If you had not been asked to update the staff, it appears that they would not have been given any direction along the way. The lack of timely instructions from you has left the system application with many empty tables, because there was not enough time for the staff to make the necessary decisions on what should be entered.

Poor planning was also evident in the area of training. Little or no time went into preparing for the staff training. On March 6th, (the first scheduled day of training) the session was cancelled. The cabling was not tested until Saturday, March 4th and was not in working order. When the training was delivered on March 7th, the Business Manager was told that the course material that was to be covered over a two day period was covered in one session.

Several times the client's work has been put on hold because of your commitments to **other** clients. This project has been negatively affected by the fact that the developer's System Analyst has not had time to deliver services in a thorough *manner, and we have not been able to count on him coming to the office as planned. The resolution of problems such as the AMS being down all day on May 1st and the loss of three applications which were installed on the network on April 30th have just had to wait until he could fit the client into his schedule. No time seems to have been allowed for him to document the User Manual and System Administrator's Guide. His time constraints appear to have gone unnoticed and have not been addressed effectively with respect to the client's needs.*

Many activities have been carried out in a disorganized manner, because tasks have continually been left half finished. This has been particularly true of the LAN installation. Enough time was not allowed for the installation of hardware, software and related applications. Consequently, there have been numerous problems and your System Analyst has spent an inordinate amount of time troubleshooting. This has left the users very frustrated with the new technology. External consultants have been brought in to evaluate the network, because the hardware environment has been so unstable.

When the installation is completed, you should provide a written report indicating that all activities listed on your December 19, 1994 fax have been completed. This report is necessary because the status of the LAN installation seems to fluctuate from day to day. In addition, time should be allocated for your System Analyst to organize the client's software and related documentation. The current condition of the client's materials is not acceptable.

Another serious problem that required a significant amount of the client's resources has been the fact that dozens of hours have had to be devoted to follow-up and research in order to resolve programming issues. There are three primary reasons for this.

First, the client has been unable to rely on the information provided by you as to what would be included in the system. Last year, the client paid to have three representatives of your company attend a meeting to discuss the second draft of the Functional Specification. The results of the meeting were not documented by anyone from your company. You have demonstrated a lack of knowledge about the client's requirements. Every request for your staff to deliver what was promised has been treated as an opportunity for "extra billings". This required the client to incur expenses to research each item to verify that it was in the Functional Specification.

When we meet this week, you should be prepared to explain why the March 14th Status Report says the Automatic Membership Cancellation Procedure is not in the Functional Specification or the information provided on the client's Checklist, particularly since these formed part of the Software Agreement.

Secondly, it has been necessary to provide in-depth explanations of the client's requirements to the programmers. I assume this is due to your misplacement of the Entity Relation Diagram. This information has already been provided to you during extensive user interviews and several meetings where the draft Specification was discussed. A considerable number of hours went into repeating this information in order to resolve problems when the programmers had made incorrect assumptions about what was required. This is why the client ended up with an inventory order form designed to support only over the counter sales. The programmer was not aware that the client does not operate a cash and carry business out of its office.

Finally, you appear to have the misconception that although the client paid $9,200.00 to translate the association's requirements into a Functional Specification document, the client should bear some responsibility for the accuracy of the technical content. The fact that the client didn't know that necessary tables and forms were left out should not justify extra billings to the client. It was not their role to verify your technical work.

Training

Your staff did not deliver training at an acceptable level. It was difficult to obtain a written plan for the training and a complete plan has never been provided, although one was requested on February 16th and March 8th. Five sessions were cancelled on short notice. On at least two occasions, staff waited in the board room for over an hour before finding out that your System Analyst would not be coming in that day. One of the reasons for cancelling the session was that he had to go to another client's site.

The staff sat through weeks of training without having the use of individual PCs, live data or any course materials. Both you and your System Analyst were advised more than once that the training was being delivered in an unacceptable manner. The situation with the PCs was brought to your attention the first time on March 8th. Your solution was to tell the staff not to worry because further training would be provided when the AMS was functional and the network was set up. Some staff were even told they didn't have to take notes. Matters were made worse by the fact that the client's busiest part of the season (membership renewal) was fast approaching.

The results achieved during the training sessions resulted in an extremely high level of frustration for the staff by the time the AMS could be accessed through the network. The initial testing was made even more difficult by the fact that the workstations were configured at different times and the information provided about the status of the network varied depending on who was asked about it.

The acceptance testing has been prolonged in part because of the poor quality of training and the fact that at least one-half of the staff did not have hardware that worked properly when the AMS could be tested. Progress reports were not provided as specified in the Software Agreement. Nor was the CEO advised that problems existed which would affect the implementation of acceptance testing.

Summary Comments

The current status of this project is completely unacceptable. Some of the AMS functions do work and the staff have received satisfactory training from the programmers; however, they are trying to perform their jobs using workarounds to problems. This cannot go on indefinitely. There is still a considerable amount of work to be done on this project. You need to document a plan for completing this work in an acceptable timeframe. Please recognize that this situation is an urgent one and requires your full attention immediately.

CHAPTER FIVE

I had an exemplary reputation when I joined the first organization as Director of Finance and Administration. I was never unemployed involuntarily. I was awarded stock options by the Board of Directors of a major computer firm, promoted four times in six years and received very good performance reviews on a consistent basis. Projects that I have managed include a building renovation valued at $200,000.00. I brought the project in on budget.

When I was no longer the Project Manager for the computer system project, the CEO did not give me a reference. Instead, she just listed the duties for which I was responsible. She did not provide any information about the quantity or quality of the work that I performed. Letters written by a past Chair of the first organization and a past President of the second organization are evidence of CEO's lies to the Boards of Directors.

To protect my reputation and that of my company I asked for a Board Review Committee to evaluate my work and agreed to settle for $11,980.79 before the disagreement became a major costly dispute. The board refused to investigate the matter. As a result, the case escalated into a multi-million dollar law suit.

In addition to unpaid consulting fees of $24,098.75, interest over a period of sixteen years at the rate of 5.5% per annum, punitive damages, legal expenses and lost profits for my company totaling $445,000.00, damages to the plaintiffs exceed one million dollars. Lost profits were calculated by a major accounting firm at a cost of $16,000.00.

Not only did the defendants ruin my reputation, but they hindered a major business opportunity to enter the software development industry for non-profit organizations. The CEO was aware of the plaintiffs' plans, signed up to participate in the project and referred potential clients to my company. My plans are supported by a detailed business plan which was evaluated by a senior partner of the accounting firm.

When the CEO refused to execute service contract **72167** without notice and ended my work on the membership system project via her June 21ˢᵗ letter, I tried to avoid problems with future references by requesting the formation of a Board Review Committee to judge the quality of all of the work I had done for the two organizations.

Good references were extremely important because of the plaintiffs' plans to enter the market for the development of software applications for the not-for-profit market. These plans had been in the works since 1993. Not only was the CEO aware of these plans, but she had signed up to participate in the plaintiffs' project.

I was forced to file a law suit against the CEO and the first organization. In the defendants' Statement of Defence and Counterclaim and Examination for Discovery, the CEO lied repeatedly. She lied and contradicted herself numerous times.

My efforts to mitigate the damages caused by the defendants include the following:

1. contacting past and present Board Directors in 1995 asking them to review my work and determine if there were any problems with the quality or the results I had achieved to date;
2. writing and calling individual directors to explain the seriousness of the problems being caused by the CEO and Agent for the association.
3. sending a request to the Board of Directors asking for partial payment ($11,980.79) for the work and services that had been provided by the plaintiffs between May 8 and May 31, 1995;
4. responding to dozens of employment advertisements and making hundreds of cold calls as part of a career counselling program that cost me $4,000.00;
5. contacting senior staff that I knew from my volunteer activities, previous jobs and previous employment applications;
6. applying for a variety of positions at all levels, both temporary and permanent;
7. putting four web sites and a video on the Internet;

8. trying every way that I could think of to make the directors on both Boards of Directors understand that I would not do anything to jeopardize my business pursuits or my reputation; and
9. writing to the editors of the Toronto Star and Globe and Mail.

CHAPTER SIX

The defendants filed a Statement of Defence and Counterclaim in response to my law suit. They are made up of nothing but lies and are contradicted by the transcript of the Examination of Discovery.

In paragraph 69 (b) of the Counterclaim the defendants claim "*damages for the Plaintiffs' failure to complete the proposal for the ongoing maintenance of the . . . computer system, estimated at $59,000.00. . . .*"

Dozens of invoices were submitted by the defendants in support of their claim. The invoices were for work requested by the CEO in addition to the computer system developer's original contract. The original contract price was $50,000.00. The additional billing was $106,387.18 for system enhancements, programming the source code, debugging the completed application and training the staff on new, added and amended system functions. The plaintiffs had no knowledge or control over the work completed by the developer after May 11, 1995.

If service contract **72167** had been executed by the CEO, it would have expired on March 31, 1996. The defendants claimed damages for work completed after March 31st, e.g., *invoice 703557 dated March 19, 1997 for general support from the developer.*

The following vendors were hired without the knowledge of the plaintiffs:

Vendor 1	*Invoice #96001*	*May 6, 1996*	*2953.20*
Vendor 1	*Invoice #96003*	*June 28, 1996*	*2974.60*
Vendor 1	*Invoice #96004*	*July 30, 1996*	*5797.60*
Vendor 1	*Invoice #96005*	*August 30, 1996*	*3509.60*
Vendor 1	*Invoice #96006*	*Sept. 30, 1996*	*3338.40*
Vendor 1	*Invoice #96007*	*October 31, 1996*	*3060.20*
Vendor 1	*Invoice #96008*	*Nov. 30, 1996*	*3289.60*
Vendor 1	*Invoice #96009*	*Dec. 31, 1996*	*1442.80*
Vendor 1	*Invoice # 97001*	*Jan. 31, 1997*	*3351.25*
Vendor 1	*Invoice #97002*	*Feb. 28, 1997*	*3490.80*
Vendor 1	*Invoice #97003*	*March 31, 1997*	*299.60*
Vendor 1	*Invoice #97004*	*April 29, 1997*	*460.10*
Vendor 1	*Invoice # 97005*	*July 16, 1997*	*160.50*
Vendor 2	*Invoice # 1708*	*Jan. 15, 1997*	*5403.50*
Vendor 2	*Invoice # 781*	*Feb. 27, 1997*	*35197.65*
Vendor 2	*Invoice # 796*	*March 27, 1997*	*20000.44*
Vendor2	*Invoice # 911*	*June 30, 1997*	*19167.61*
Vendor 3	*Account 268538*	*Aug. 28, 1997*	*11621.68*
Vendor 4	*Invoice 970531*	*May 31, 1997*	*3638.00*

The CEO incurred the following expenses after I was no longer Project Manager for the computer system:

| Vendor 5 | Invoice 1205 | May 31, 1995 | 341.06 |
| Vendor 5 | Invoice 1211 | June 30, 1995 | 160.50 |

Vendor 6 (developer) GST excluded

Invoice	505204	May 20, 1995	5850.00
	506217	June 24, 1995	3500.00
	506218	June 24, 1995	3300.00
	506219	June 24, 1995	3186.23
	506220	June 24, 1995	1635.00
	507229	July 26, 1995	1290.00
	507230	July 26, 1995	2630.40
	507231	July 26, 1995	2925.00
	509249	Sept. 4, 1995	2742.50
	509250	Sept. 4, 1995	1377.50
	509251	Sept. 4, 1995	1355.40
	509255	Sept. 4, 1995	2081.25
	510272	Oct. 7, 1995	425.00
	510273	Oct. 7, 1995	3147.06
	510274	Oct. 7, 1995	1211.63
	510288	Oct. 22, 1995	2169.56
	511311	Nov. 27, 1995	5074.50
	512319	Dec. 10, 1995	4694.50
	512323	Dec. 11, 1995	1394.12
	601331	Jan. 14, 1996	3105.75
	602352	Feb. 11, 1996	7249.00
	603364	March 9, 1996	4267.25
	604375	April 13, 1996	3871.75

605386	*May 20, 1996*	*4886.88*
605392	*June 1, 1996*	*8367.38*
607501	*July 10, 1996*	*3831.00*
608509	*Aug. 28, 1996*	*2588.00*
609517	*Sept. 7, 1996*	*2142.75*
610524	*Oct. 14, 1996*	*7523.00*
611531	*Nov. 12, 1996*	*347.25*
612537	*Dec. 15, 1996*	*234.25*
703557	*March 19, 1997*	*998.50*

CHAPTER SEVEN

In paragraph 61 of their Counterclaim, the defendants state that ". . . *without notice or cause, the Plaintiffs withdrew their services from the Project resulting in delays and re-work of many of the tasks which were the responsibility of the Plaintiffs.*"

Per my Letter of Engagement dated April 4, 1995, there were no tasks to be reworked. The letter states:

"As Project Coordinator, I will handle the following tasks:

1. *Chair meetings of the Working Group and provide support to complete follow-up activities identified during the meetings.*
2. *Monitor the status of activities assigned to team members with respect to meeting deadlines and advise the CEO of any missed deadlines.*
3. *By January 31, 1996, prepare a Policy Document . . . which documents the historical development of the National Membership Management System, how the System will be maintained/updated on an ongoing basis and the decision making process that has been agreed upon by all project participants.*

> 4. *By January 31, 1996, document an evaluation process
> to obtain feedback from provincial organizations on
> the quality of and member satisfaction with services
> provided . . . under the national system."*

Number one could not be done because the CEO cancelled
the June 14, 1995 meeting without notice. Number
two was an ongoing process involving both written and
verbal notices to the CEO. Number three was completed
as a draft per the usual process followed by the Working
Group. An evaluation process was documented as a draft
and was submitted to the CEO on June 9, 1995.

In paragraph 63 of the Counterclaim the defendants state:
". . . . *the Plaintiffs undertook to provide . . . a proposal
for the ongoing administration of the new computer system
being installed at the . . . offices."*

This was a lie. What the plaintiffs did propose was a new
service contract on March 31, 1995, number **72167**.
Per the defendants Statement of Defence, paragraph 14,
"The draft contract,. . . identified as service contract **72167**,
*was not executed by" the CEO "or any authorized employee,
director or officer of the" organization "at any time. Further,
at no time did" the CEO "or any authorized employee,
director or officer of the" organization "verbally agree to the
terms set out in service contract* **72167**."

Without a signed contract, the plaintiffs were not
obligated to provide any services for the defendants,
including a proposal for the ongoing administration of
the new computer system. The CEO stated the following
while under oath at the Examination for Discovery:

At questions 149 through 151 of the transcript of Discovery, the CEO lied again. She was asked if she requested the plaintiff to develop a plan for the ongoing administration of the computer system and to put it in writing . . . She answered "yes." She was asked if she had . . . the document on file. She answered, *"There was no plan. There was what you've called service contract 72167—this is what was provided in my request to" prepare "a proposal or plan for the ongoing administration of the system."* This makes no sense since the service contract draft was given to the CEO with my March 31, 1995 final project report.

On March 9, 1995, I provided the CEO with a written interim progress report for the computer system project. On page four, I outlined the available options for future system support. Option (c) was as follows:

My company *"can provide a System Analyst for two days (14 hours) a week at the rate of $45,000 per year. Additional hours would be billed at the rate of $50 per hour. The cost of a contract covering the period of June 1, 1995 to March 31, 1996 would be $37,500. If the contract can be billed in advance on the first of each month, June 1st to March 1st, I can provide a System Analyst for 88 hours during the month of May 1995 at no charge to the organization. This would facilitate a smooth takeover from the developer. My first choice for this position is Dave Marsh. I have attached his résumé for your reference."*

On March 31, 1995 I provided the CEO with a written final project report for the computer system. On page two under outstanding action items, number three states: "*I have attached a draft contract for" my company "to provide a System Analyst for" your organization. "Dave Marsh has accepted another position. If I cannot confirm who will be filling this job by April 10th, I will provide the individual's résumé for your approval and arrange for a meeting when you return to the office."*

As of April 24th, the defendants and plaintiffs had not come to an agreement on service contract **72167.** I had several concerns about the scope of the contract. I wrote a letter to the CEO on April 24th about my contract proposal and my leaving the project as Project Manager. I wrote the following:

"April 24, 1995

Dear :

. . . I have prepared a status report on the system implementation for you and MAR. Please advise me if you wish me to continue providing support until May 5th, assuming the AMS is accepted by that date. All of the activities identified in the status report do not necessarily need to be performed by me. I recommend that you and MAR take over working with the individual staff during the week of May 1st. This would provide two important benefits, i.e., minimize additional expenses for my services, and provide both of you with the information that you will need to make realistic assessments of your ongoing support needs for the balance of the year.

*Based on my experience during this implementation, I do not believe that part-time support is appropriate. Consequently, **I***

will not be pursuing my previous contract proposal . . . I would appreciate it if you could let me know what you plan to do by May 5ᵗʰ . . ."

On April 25ᵗʰ, I met with the CEO to discuss my concerns. We agreed that I would revise the contract and resubmit it to her, which I did on or about May 5th. I signed the contract on May 8ᵗʰ. I also hired a System Analyst, who started work supporting three organizations on May 8ᵗʰ.

At question 166 of the Discovery transcript the CEO states that she ". . . was aware" my employee "was" working at her organization "under the provisions of this service contract **72167**."

According to the financial rules of the first organization, the CEO cannot bind the organization to verbal contracts. During Discovery, the CEO claimed at question 167 of the transcript that ". . . *I never signed the contract; we only agreed to the details within the contract . . .*" This was a lie. At paragraph 14 of the Statement of Defence, the CEO stated ". . . *at no time did*" the CEO "*or any authorized employee, director or officer of the*" organization "*verbally agree to the terms set out in service contract* **72167**."

In paragraph 68 of the defendants' Statement of Defence, the CEO states: ". . . *the Plaintiffs' actions were designed to harm the Defendants' reputation, frustrate the attempts of*" the CEO "*to follow her mandate from the Board of Directors and to further complicate and delay the completion of the installation of the computer system.*" This statement is ludicrous given the magnitude of what I had to lose by jeopardizing the success of this project, and the fact that I gave the CEO more than a month's notice of termination of my work as Project Manager.

Per my report (AMS Implementation Status Report) dated April 24, 1995, I engaged an individual certified by Novelle as an expert in local area networks to inspect the entire network configuration and to correct any deficiencies prior to the first organization accepting the system from the developer. I did this at my own expense to minimize the chance ". . . of the" organization "encountering major problems with the network soon after the AMS was accepted."

My project reports are proof that I made every effort to minimize problems and worked tirelessly to make sure that this project was completed successfully. In paragraph 27 of the Statement of Defence, the CEO states: ". . . *the relationship between the Plaintiffs and the*" organization "*was terminated by the Plaintiffs without notice or cause.*" This is another ludicrous lie, since I had been working for the defendants free of charge since May 12, 1995. In addition, I provided a System Analyst to support staff of three organizations full-time. Without a service contract in place, the defendants could hardly expect me and my company to continue to provide services.

At question 216 of the transcript of Discovery, the CEO accused the plaintiffs of walking out on the project without notice. She had in fact committed fraud. She waited until May 30th to say that she would not be executing service contract **72167.** I had worked for free from May 12th through May 30th under the belief that my contract had been executed. I had also provided a

System Analyst full-time for $3,000.00 from May 8th through May 31st.

Even though the CEO had been the Project Manager for the computer system project since May 12th, at question 216 of the transcript of Examination for Discovery, she claimed that the plaintiffs were responsible for managing the project. She stated *". . . When they walked out without notice . . . we had to find without any notice people to manage and maintain a computer system that was not operational and not fully developed."* The plaintiffs were not responsible for developing reports. Per the May 8th deficiency report to the developer, they were solely responsible for problems with the development of reports. In addition, I gave written notice of the termination of my services on April 3, 1995. I wrote the CEO the following letter:

"April 3, 1995

Dear :

Attached is the final report on work performed on the "computer system development project covered by contract 72850. I have included information on job tasks which must be handled by" the "staff or contract personnel. The outstanding work which must be completed by the developer and updates for some of the action items listed in my last Interim Project Report" is decribed.

In the future, I will provide services on a time and materials basis at the rate of seventy-five ($75) dollars per hour. At the present time, I am planning to provide support for a maximum of 125 hours up to May 5th . . . .

Noie James

Please let me know if you require any additional information or have any questions.

Sincerely

Consultant"

I worked until May 8th, in order to meet with the developer and the CEO about the project deficiency report. She did not ask me to continue my role as Project Manager. Instead, she took over and approved the developer going over budget.

At questions 252 and 253 of the transcript of the Examination for Discovery, the defendants' solicitor lied on behalf of the CEO by reiterating her previous lies under oath. He stated *". . . the Plaintiffs did provide service . . . and the terms of that loose agreement—some of the terms of the proposal of the Plaintiffs were incorporated into that loose arrangement. . . . My understanding is that it was a verbal agreement between"* the plaintiffs and the defendants *"that the verbal agreement in fact did reflect some of the proposals in the document numbered 72167."*

Question 267 asked by the plaintiffs' solicitor was "So when . . ." the parties didn't "come to an agreement on 72167" what was the "expectation of the work" the plaintiffs "were obligated to perform?"

The defendants' solicitor replied ". . . The expectation was that the proposal 72167 would be negotiated to the point that it would become a contract and the claim that we're making is that it was the withdrawal of services without notice or cause so that the defendants were in a position of having to find other suppliers on an emergency basis almost to make up for the deficiencies of the plaintiffs' work and also to complete the work that the plaintiffs represented that they would perform."

The letter from the CEO to the plaintiff dated May 30, 1995 does not reflect any work left undone by the plaintiffs or significant problems caused by the plaintiffs declining to continue to work for free without a signed contract.

The CEO wrote in her letter that "*I would like to thank you for the documentation and planning that you did to focus the computer project on outstanding issues and requirements and for providing for contingencies. We did make the decision to install the new version of forms software and we did have" the programmers "redo all the forms in the system. Work on reports is progressing, although more slowly than hoped.*

. . . I regret that the contract you were proposing did not turn out better."

CHAPTER EIGHT

The defendants' Examination for Discovery took place on September 14, 2000. The defendants' solicitor followed up on November 3 and November 21, 2000. I responded to his letters on November 28th.

I submitted a detailed list of additional questions and a request for specific documents. The defendants refused to complete Discovery. The CEO swore a false affidavit stating "... *At this time, there have been no further Discoveries of either party arising out of the written questions and answers. ... I believe that the Discoveries in this matter are now complete ...*" The defendant and the defendants' solicitor lied to the court in a Motion submitted to the court on December 5, 2000.

I posed new questions and requested copies of numerous documents. The defendants did not reply to my letter or comply with my requests.

I wrote the following letter to the defendants' solicitor on November 28, 2000:

"Dear Mr. :

. . . The following information relates to the defendant's written responses to the plaintiffs written questions and to questions answered by the defendant at the Examination for Discovery on September 14, 2000.

*Which terms and conditions of service contract **72167** is the defendant claiming were not binding on both the defendants and the plaintiffs? Is the defendant claiming that no additional terms and conditions were binding on both parties other than those documented in service contract **72167** dated May 8, 1995?*

Provide a copy of the complete Board Policy document that was in effect on May 30, 1995 (including the revised policy IV E Executive Limitations, Asset Protection, pages one and two) approved by the Board of Directors on February 20, 1994 . . .

The defendant's answer to my question eight is incomplete. Pursuant to Rule 31.06 (2) of the Rules of Civil Procedure, provide the names, addresses and telephone numbers of each person identified in the defendant's answer. In addition to the Board meeting minutes for November 8, 1995, provide the names, addresses and telephone numbers of each person who was present at the meeting referenced by the defendant in Schedule B of the defendants' Affidavit of Documents dated October 15, 1997.

. . . With respect to the defendants' provision of a further and better Affidavit of Documents pursuant to Rule 30.06 (b), I am requesting that the following information be provided:

*a copy of the revised Policy Document dated June 14, 1995 and referenced at paragraph 44 of the defendants' Statement of Defence; copies of invoices and the related documentation or evidence for the work on the Membership System project that the" staff "was required to re-do as referenced . . . in paragraph 61 of the defendants' Counterclaim ["The Defendants state that, without notice or cause, <u>the Plaintiffs</u> withdrew their services from the Project resulting in delays and re-work of many of the tasks <u>which were the responsibility of the Plaintiffs"].</u> NOTE: Evidence supporting the claim for $6,350.00 in damages referenced at paragraph 69 (a) of the Counterclaim was never provided.; copies of any and all documentation regarding the responsibilities and names of the project team members for the period August 1994 through May 11, 1995 . . ." a copy of the outsourcing agreement prepared by vendor 3; and details of all work that the defendants are claiming damages for, that was not outside of the scope of the plaintiffs' service contract **72167** . . . ."*

CHAPTER NINE

Because the defendants did not complete Discovery, the case could not be set down for trial. On December 5, 2000, the parties' Motion and response were not dealt with. Instead, the Judge ordered the plaintiffs to retain counsel in order to continue with the case.

As of March 5, 2001, the plaintiffs were still without counsel. Justice Jenkins dismissed the plaintiffs claim with permission to re-file the claim. He rendered his Order on the basis that the matter had been before the court for six years. He stated that he deemed the dispute to be primarily about money. He attempted to move the matter along and on to trial. He ordered that the plaintiffs could file a claim for an amount up to $25,000.00 without legal representation. He also ordered that the plaintiffs could file a claim in superior court for damages in excess of $25,000.00 provided they were represented by counsel.

The Order reads as follows:

"Order to issue permission for" the plaintiff "to represent" her company "to the extent of her claims for loss of earnings pursuant to the alleged contract which cannot exceed $25,000.00. The plaintiff is given leave to launch a new action if she deems it sagacious to claim whatever other relief she seeks, such as damages for loss of ability to obtain other employment contracts, libel and slander, or other remedies she considers appropriate. Such future action is subject to the usual defences that the defendant considers appropriate."

No costs were assessed and at no time was the plaintiffs claim judged to be without merit.

When the plaintiffs re-filed the claims, Justice Jenkins Order was overruled at two subsequent motion hearings. The plaintiffs' request was dismissed at both hearings, primarily because the judges did not agree that the plaintiffs should be allowed to pursue the same case in the courts more than once. This was a travesty of justice because the plaintiffs never had a chance to go to trial.

CHAPTER TEN

My attempt to get justice through the legal system was a complete failure. The defendants took every opportunity to delay the litigation process. It took the CEO eight weeks to reply to seven written questions submitted to the defendants' solicitor. The answers were not complete. The defendants refused to complete Discovery, did not respond to four interrogatories and did not complete both undertakings.

Between the defendants' deliberate delays and the court delays, the case was before the courts for more than six years. There were more than ten motion hearings starting in September 1999. Each time we went to court, we appeared before a different Judge or Justice who had not read the motion records beforehand. On one occasion, the defendants' solicitor left the courthouse before our matter was called. The motion was put over to another week.

The defendants' solicitor lied in his Factum presented to the court on December 5, 2000 in order to avoid completing the defendants' Examination for Discovery. The judges would get side tracked and wouldn't deal with the motions in front of them. One judge ordered that both sides submit a one page summary of the issues to the court. The summary was not dealt with by the next judge.

By 2003, the plaintiffs had exhausted their financial resources. As a result, the defendants and plaintiffs agreed to a Full and Final Mutual Release. The plaintiffs signed the release February 3, 2003.

Although the release was meant to avoid further litigation, there was never an agreement by the plaintiffs to discontinue every effort to restore the plaintiffs' good name and reputation.

Under the circumstances and in the face of incontrovertible proof of immoral behavior by the CEO, the Boards of Directors of the organizations and sponsors have a moral obligation to determine the truth about this disagreement.

I believe that by supporting the two organizations, sponsors should be considered to be complicit in the amoral behavior of the defendants. Sponsors should encourage the formation of a Board Review Committee. Besides obtaining financial compensation, my goals for this book include the dismissal of the CEO for immoral and illegal behavior.